Allah is My Lord

By Umm Assad

This book belongs to

ISBN-13:
ISBN-10:

Author   Umm Assad Bint Jamil Mohammed
Illustrator   A. Revello
Co-Illustrators   R. Bufao, Umm Assad
Book Design   Umm Assad Bint Jamil Mohammed
Editor   C. Cutting
Published on   2017CE/1438H

ummassadpublications.com

Bismillahir-Rahmanir-Raheem. Indeed, all praise is for Allah. We praise Him; we seek His help, and we seek His Forgiveness. We seek refuge with Allah from the evil of our own souls and the consequence of our actions. Whomsoever Allah guides, nobody can misguide and whomsoever Allah misguides nobody can guide. I testify that none has the right to be worshipped except Allah alone, He has no partners, and I testify that Muhammad is His slave and Messenger.

DEDICATION

My dear Mother and Father
whom I could never ever repay
My inspiring children
Whom I hope to inspire someday
My loving husband
Who has been with me all the way
And all those I forgot to mention
I make a Dua for you this day:

"May Allah give us glad tidings of peace and tranquillity for eternity. Ameen."

Umm Assad

Allah is the only Lord and the creator of us all.[1]
He created the world around me and provided for it all.[2]

Some things that we can see and some things not at all.[3]
The sun, moon, stars and galaxy. Alhamdulillah for it all.[4]

Some things are very big and some things are very small.
Like this big tree in the park and the little fruits that fall.

I want to see the whole wide world and travel through it all.
I really want to fly up high and see the waterfall.

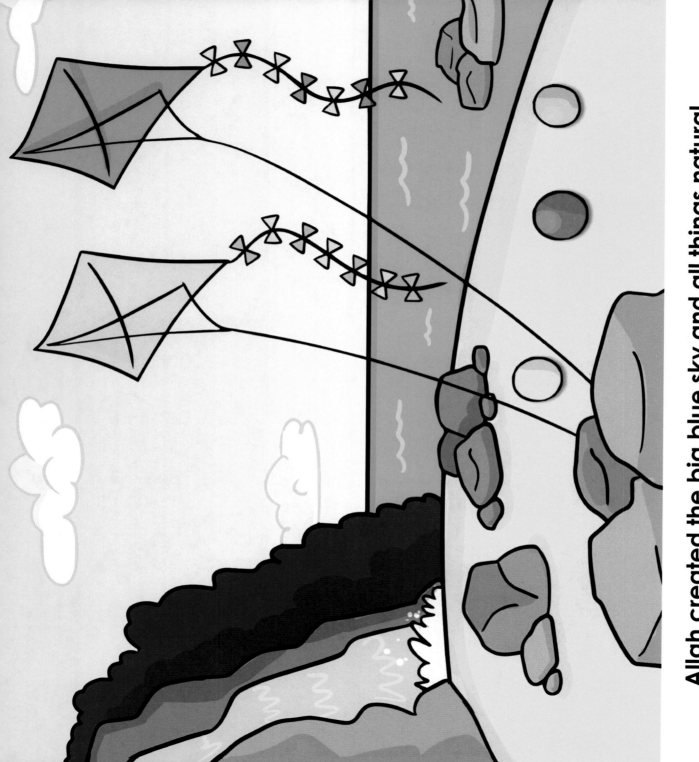

Allah created the big blue sky and all things natural.
He created all the rocks and seas. They look so beautiful.

I learn about the world outside. It's all so wonderful.
The mountains, trees and flowers are all so colourful.5

Allah created the people. 6 Some black, white, short or tall.
So many different countries yet Allah is the Lord of us all.

No matter where we are, Allah can See us all.
Everything we say, Allah can Hear it all. [7]

Allah created the animals. Some fly, walk, swim or crawl.[8]
They live among the land and sea. I'd like to see them all.

I learn about them all day long to remind me of my Lord.
He created everything in pairs.⁹ Allah created them all.

Allah created the materials. There are so many useful tools.
They help us to build the furniture in our homes and schools.

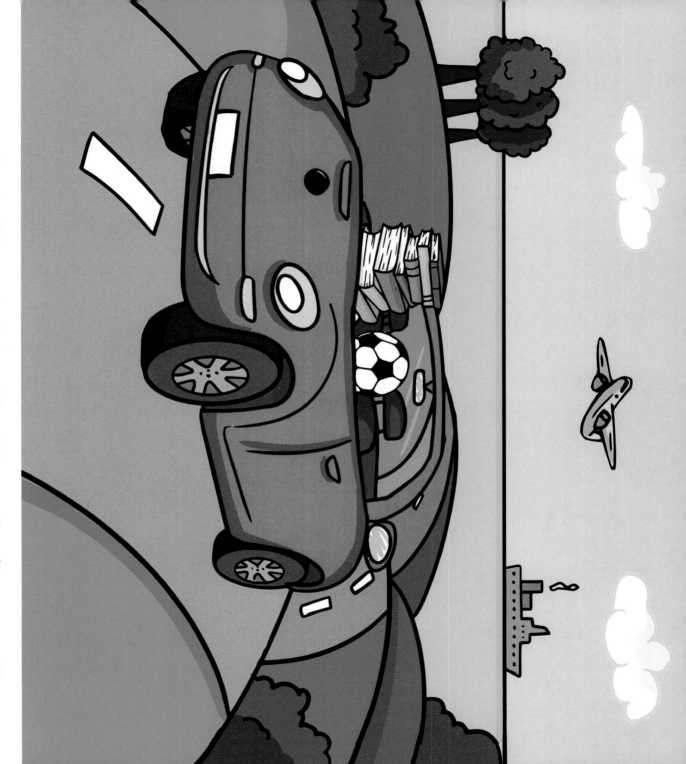

We also build our transport to ride and sail or soar.[10]
So many things we own like our toys and books and more.

Food and drink to give us energy from the early morn.
All our modest clothing and our shoes that can be worn.

I'm grateful for my dinner. I always eat it all.[1]
I have five senses to explore. Alhamdulillah for it all.

Allah created the time. We move from dusk to dawn.[12]
He is aware of everything, even before we were born.[13]

Allah created the weather. It's either cold or warm.[14] He created all the colours and every lightning storm.

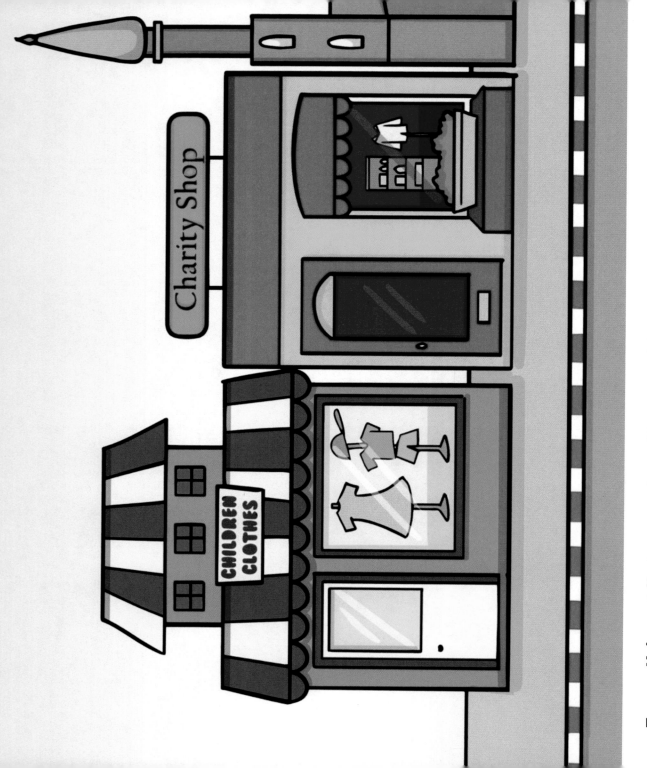

Everything Allah creates, He provides enough for it all.[15] He takes care of our health and wealth, whether rich or poor.

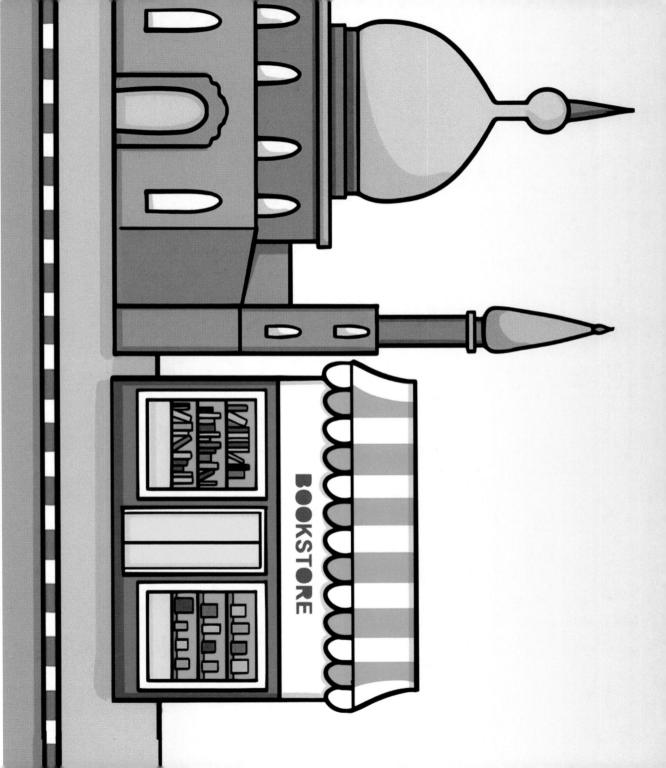

To have fear in Allah alone is the best provision of all.[16]
So be patient, grateful and repent to the one and only Lord.

He guided us to Islam.[17] He is so Merciful.
We read and learn about Him in books which are truthful.

All praise is to Allah, the Lord of all the worlds.
The Lord of all His creation, all the boys and girls. [18]

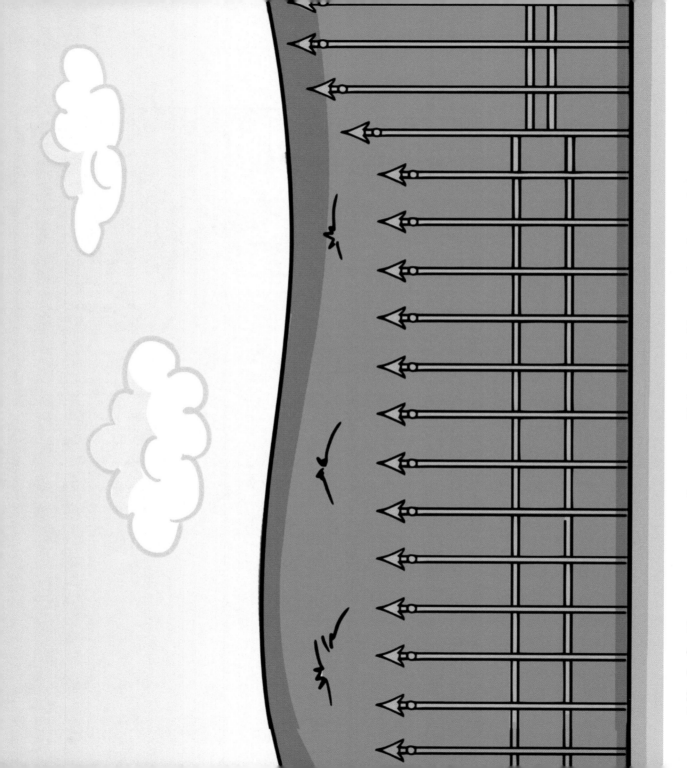

Allah is the owner of everything in the whole wide world.[19] Someday we will return to Him, whether young or old.[20]

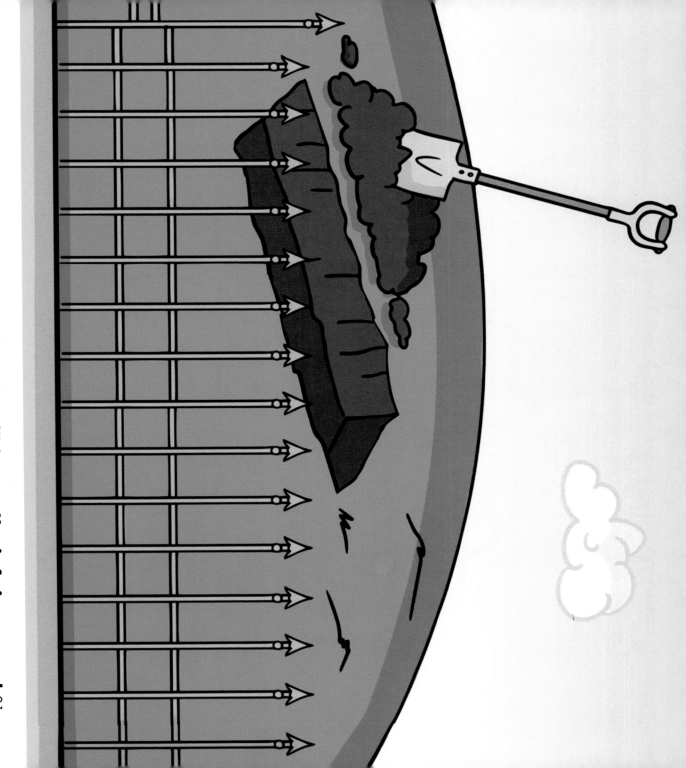

All our good and bad deeds will have their fair reward.[21]
Muslims go to Jannah, a place where no one's bored.

It's full of fun and laughter and peace forevermore. 22
It's better and longer-lasting than all we've sensed before.

Someday I hope to go there with the people I adore, like my family and my friends, to see our one and only Lord.[23]

But until that day I won't forget what I was created for.
It's to worship Allah alone, learn about Islam and more.[24]

Allah is my only Lord, The Creator, The Provider and The Owner of us all. Someday we will all return to Him…

Say, "Alhamdulillah for it all."

Glossary

Allah: The Name of The One True God.
Alhamdulillah: All praise is due to Allah.
Jannah: Paradise.
Muslim: The one who worships Allah alone.
Tawheed: Allah is the only Lord of creation. He alone is the provider and sustainer. Allah has Names and Attributes that none of the creation share and Allah is to be singled out for worship, alone. Tawheed is maintaining the Oneness of Allah in all the above mentioned categories. Islam makes a clear distinction between the Creator and the created.
Al-Khaaliq: The Creator.
Ar-Razzaaq: The Provider.
Al-Malik: The Owner of the Dominion.
Rabb: The Lord.

Endnotes

1. Quran: Surah 1, Ayah 2/Surah 2, Ayah 21/Surah 6, Ayah 1, Ayah 101-102
2. Quran: Surah 2, Ayah 22/Surah 51, Ayah 56-58/Surah 34, Ayah 24/Surah 39, Ayah 62
3. Quran: Surah 6, Ayah 59
4. Quran: Surah 41, Ayah 37/Surah 7, Ayah 54/Surah 31, Ayah 25
5. Quran: Surah 88, Ayah 17-21/Surah 21, Ayah 31-33/Surah 56, Ayah 63-72
6. Quran: Surah 49, Ayah 13/Surah 23, Ayah 14/Surah 51, Ayah 56/Surah 67, Ayah 2/Surah 6, Ayah 2 /Surah 7, Ayah 11/Surah 55, Ayah 14/Surah 52, Ayah 35-36
7. Quran: Surah 40, Ayah 20
8. Quran: Surah 24, Ayah 45
9. Quran: Surah 51, Ayah 49/Surah 42, Ayah 11/Surah 11, Ayah 40
10. Quran: Surah 10, Ayah 22/Surah 11, Ayah 37
11. Quran: Surah 16, Ayah 114
12. Quran: Surah 41, Ayah 37, Surah 21, Ayah 33
13. Quran: Surah 6, Ayah 59
14. Quran: Surah 25, Ayah 48-50
15. Quran: Surah 13, Ayah 16 (Also see endnote 2)
16. Quran: Surah 2, Ayah 197/Surah 69, Ayah 48
17. Quran: Surah 5, Ayah 3/Surah 30, Ayah 30
18. Quran: Surah 1, Ayah 1
19. Quran: Surah 25, Ayah 2/Surah 4, Ayah 131/Surah 67, Ayah 1/Surah 3, Ayah 26/Surah 31, Ayah 26
20. Quran: Surah 29, Ayah 5/Surah 18, Ayah 110/Surah 10, Ayah 31
21. Quran: Surah 99, Ayah 4-8
22. Quran: Surah 32, Ayah 17/Surah 44, Ayah 51-57/Surah 13, Ayah 23-24
23. Quran: Surah 41, Ayah 30-32
24. Quran: Surah 51, Ayah 56

Note: For more references, please refer to authentic sources.

ABOUT THE AUTHOR:

Umm Assad grew up in London, in a large and reserved Muslim family. She cared for the elderly and pre-school children in much of her early employment and studied at a College where she obtained a health and social care diploma.

In 2003, Umm Assad travelled to the Middle East where she lived for a year. During this time, she improved her Arabic and Islamic Education, believing that the only way to gain correct Islamic knowledge is by using authentic sources and referring to the real Scholars.

One of her favourite sayings is by Scholar Muhammed ibn Sireen; *'this knowledge is a matter of deen (religion) so be careful who you take your deen from.'*

From early childhood, she had a great love for helping others, seeking knowledge and writing to express her lessons in life. Over the years, this passion has seen her create unique books, children's educational resources and even poetry of which some she now enjoys sharing.

Umm Assad now has a family of her own where she home-schools all her children and even set up her own children's homeschool group at home.

You can contact Umm Assad where you can also download your free 'Islamic Activity Pack' to use alongside her books:

Websites: ummassadpublications.com, ummassadhomeschool.com
Twitter: ummassadpubs
Instagram: ummassad.pubs
Facebook: ummassadpubs
Youtube: ummassadpublications

ummassadpublications.com

'Take Pride in Authenticity'

Made in the USA
Middletown, DE
02 May 2021